Coming Home For Christmas

ADVENT IN ISAIAH

1517.

1517.

Coming Home For Christmas

ADVENT IN ISAIAH

Coming Home For Christmas

ADVENT IN ISAIAH

1517 Advent Devotional

WRITTEN AND EDITED BY

1517.

Table of Contents

Introduction

The book of Isaiah spans one of the most turbulent periods in Israel's history. Isaiah prophesied during the 8th century B.C., a time when the once-unified kingdom of Israel had divided into the northern kingdom (Israel) and the southern kingdom (Judah). As Assyria's power surged across the ancient Near East, the northern kingdom fell to its armies in 722 B.C. Meanwhile, Judah watched anxiously as the threat of foreign domination grew.

Isaiah's ministry in the capital of Judah, Jerusalem, spanned the reigns of several kings, including Uzziah, Jotham, Ahaz, and Hezekiah (Isa. 1:1). He warned Judah about the consequences of their idolatry, injustice, and misplaced trust in political alliances rather than in the Lord. His early prophecies focus on coming judgment, yet they are also laced with hope, most famously in the promise of *Immanuel*, "God with us" (Isa. 7:14).

The later chapters of Isaiah reflect a shift in tone and timeline, addressing a people either in exile or anticipating it. By then, Assyria had waned, and Babylon had risen to dominate the region, eventually conquering Jerusalem and carrying many Judeans into exile in 586 B.C. These later chapters speak with extraordinary hope about God's power to redeem, restore, and bring his people home through this Immanuel, his one and only son, Jesus.

It is Jesus, the incarnation of the living God, who Isaiah promised would come as a child born, a son given (Isa. 9:7). Jesus, the holy seed (Isa. 6:13) from the root of Jesse (Isa. 11:10), who would go to the cross for our sake: "being despised and rejected" and "pierced for our transgressions; crushed for our iniquities" (Isa. 53:3,5). Amid exile, Isaiah prophesied only one way home to our God: through the arrival of the God-man, Jesus.

Whether you use this as a personal devotional or in a group setting, we pray that this short study in Isaiah strengthens your faith in the ultimate Christmas gift, Jesus Christ. He is our shelter in the storm, our warmth in the waiting, and our welcome in the wandering. Our exile finally ends through Jesus, for he is our Home.

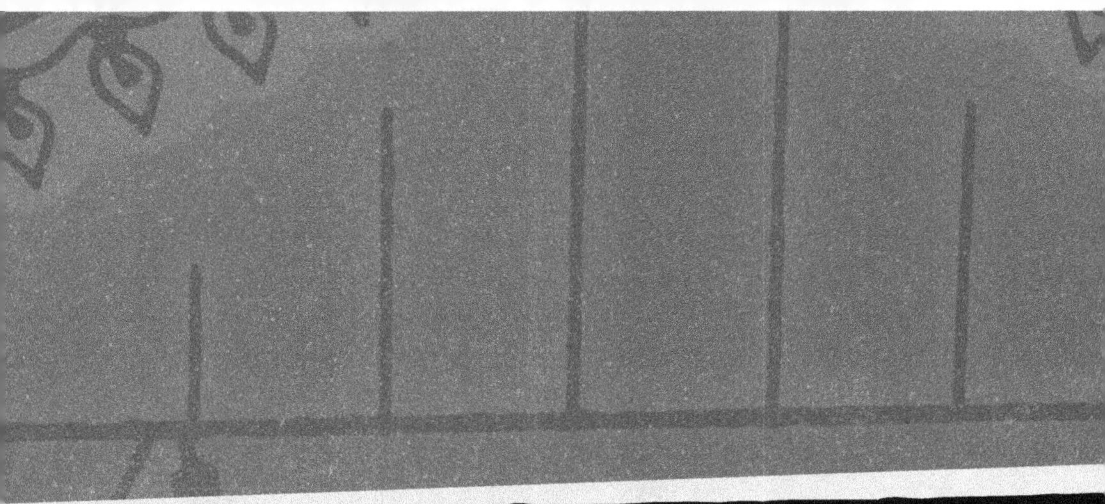

“

He is our shelter in the storm, our warmth in the waiting, and our welcome in the wandering. Our exile finally ends through Jesus, for he is our Home.

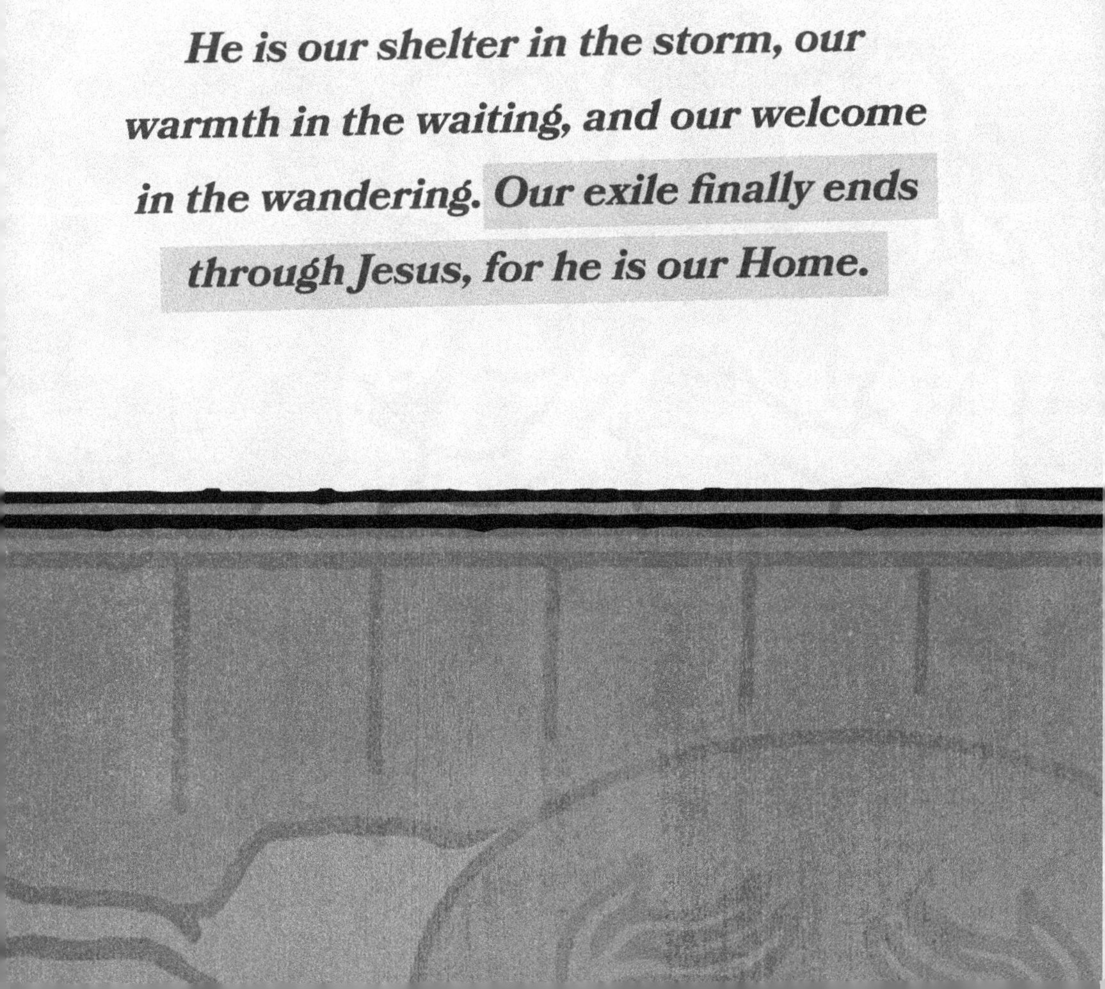

Coming Home For Christmas

ADVENT IN ISAIAH

Advent and Christmas Sermon Series

Mountains of Peace

ISAIAH 2:1-5

The word that Isaiah the son of Amoz saw concerning Judah and Jerusalem. It shall come to pass in the latter day that the mountain of the house of the Lord shall be established as the highest of the mountains, and shall be lifted up above the hills; and all the nations shall flow to it, and many peoples shall come, and say: "Come, let us go up to the mountain of the Lord, to the house of the God of Jacob, that he may teach us his ways and that we may walk in his paths." For out of Zion shall go forth the law, and the word of the Lord from Jerusalem He shall judge between the nations, and shall decide disputes for many peoples; and they shall beat their swords into plowshares, and their spears into pruning hooks; nation shall not lift up sword against nation, neither shall they learn war anymore. O house of Jacob, come, let us walk in the light of the Lord.

"Start at the beginning, and when you get to the end–stop" is good advice for the reading and writing of books, as Lewis Carrol knew so well. However, Isaiah is not an author who plays by the rules. Instead of starting at the beginning, he jumps right to the end: "In the last days," he says in verse 2. The picture he goes on to paint is nothing short of breathtaking, illustrated in both earthly and divine hues.

Isaiah begins with a mountain range, where one peak soars head-and-shoulders above the rest. Over the years, many rivers and streams have carved their way into this particular mountainside, rivers of every imaginable size, shape, color, depth, and volume. But there is also something strange about these rivers, and as we look closer at Isaiah's painting, we see it: These rivers are flowing upward, toward the peak! Their waters are drawn toward the top by an unseen force.

Isaiah pictures Mount Zion–which is both the physical location of the Temple Mount and the symbolic representation of God's rule and reign (i.e., his Kingdom) as a city on a hill toward which all people will one day flow. Mount Zion becomes the spiritual confluence point where all tribes and tongues and nations will meet to form one river, “a river whose streams make glad the city of God” (Isa. 46:4).

But perhaps most surprisingly is what’s happening at the peak of Mount Zion. Unlike Israel’s pagan neighbors, whose deities were said to fight bloody battles atop nearby Mount Zaphon, Mount Zion is a place of peace. Here, swords are transformed into plows and spears re-fashioned into pruning hooks. The agricultural imagery takes us back to Genesis 2. **On Zion’s peak, we hear echoes of Eden, where believers enjoy peace with God and peace with one another.** No more sin. No more curse. No more death. No more sorrow. And all because, through Jesus Christ, we have finally arrived at a true and better Zion (Heb. 12:22-24).

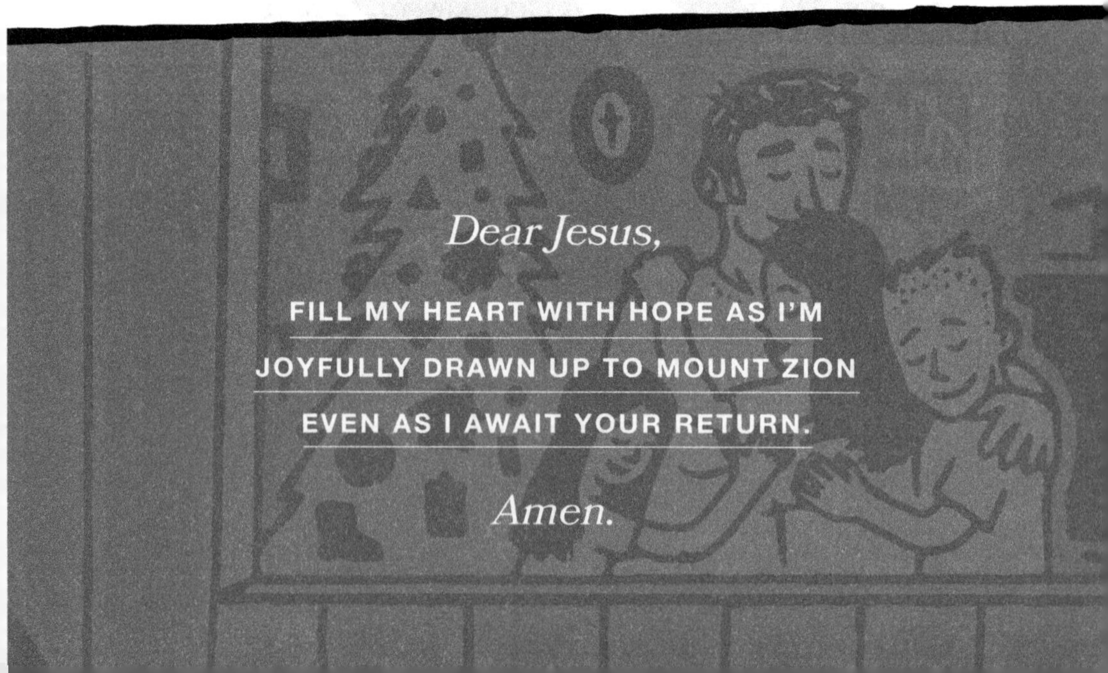

Dear Jesus,

FILL MY HEART WITH HOPE AS I’M
JOYFULLY DRAWN UP TO MOUNT ZION
EVEN AS I AWAIT YOUR RETURN.

Amen.

Our Flesh and Blood God

ISAIAH 7:10-14

Again the Lord spoke to Ahaz: "Ask a sign of the Lord your God; let it be deep as Sheol or high as heaven." But Ahaz said, "I will not ask, and I will not put the Lord to the test." And he said, "Hear then, O house of David! Is it too little for you to weary men, that you weary my God also? Therefore the Lord himself will give you a sign. Behold, the virgin shall conceive and bear a son, and shall call his name Immanuel.

The name Immanuel comes from two Hebrew words: Immanu ("with us") and El ("God"). It means "God with us." Long before Jesus was born, God promised to be with his people. He told Isaac and Jacob, "I am with you" (Gen. 26:24; 28:15), and assured Moses at the burning bush, "I will be with you" (Exod. 3:12).

But through Isaiah, God foretold a day when he would not be just spiritually present but physically present, too: "Behold, the virgin shall conceive and bear a son, and shall call his name Immanuel" (v. 14).

It's one thing for God to be with us as God; it's another for him to become human—developing in the womb, learning to walk, going through puberty, and facing crucifixion. That is Jesus: truly God, truly man.

He is your Immanuel. He knows what it's like to weep, to bleed, to be loved and betrayed. No emotion or pain is foreign to him. The image-maker became the image; the Creator became a creature. He is the God who chose to humble himself, entering the imperfect and fallenness of your home, in order to bring you home to himself.

As Immanuel, he's the best-behaved (and yet thoroughly surprising and uninvited) house guest you could ask for. He dwells with us and yet he also declares our current home is in need of improvement. And so he gets to work doing just that, through his word he remakes us and gives us his righteousness.

All this he has the power to do since he reigns with all authority in heaven and on earth—and he exercises that authority for us. He makes himself at home in our mess and he's more than aware of all of our faults: he's closer than a brother, a friend who never leaves our side, after all.

Imagine the most powerful person in the world. They have the influence to make things happen, and happen quickly. Everyone around them yields to their authority. Now imagine that person is couch surfing in your home. If you need something, they are there. If you need a favor, they can act immediately. Even that pales in comparison to what we have in Jesus. He is the Creator. He is King. He is Lord. And he dwells with us.

If you ever wonder how far God would go to make you his own and draw you into the warmth of his hospitality, where he has said you belong forever, look down into the humble home of the stable and up at the cross. That's your answer.

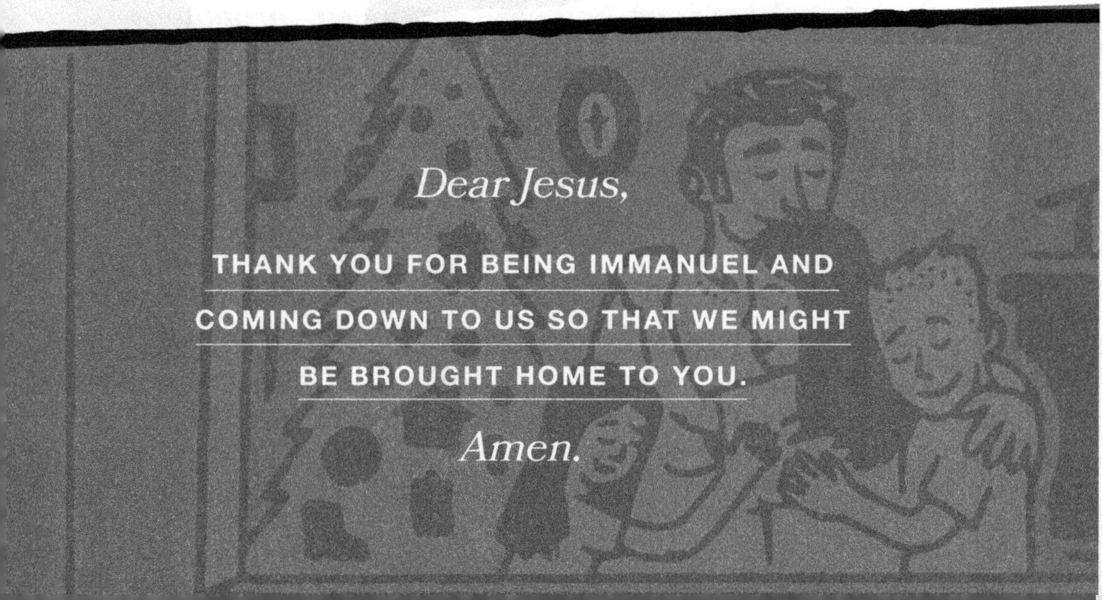

Dear Jesus,

THANK YOU FOR BEING IMMANUEL AND COMING DOWN TO US SO THAT WE MIGHT BE BROUGHT HOME TO YOU.

Amen.

Burning Bloody Boots

ISAIAH 9:1-5

But there will be no gloom for her who was in anguish. In the former time he brought into contempt the land of Zebulun and the land of Naphtali, but in the latter time he has made glorious the way of the sea, the land beyond the Jordan, Galilee of the nations.

The people who walked in darkness have seen a great light; those who dwelt in a land of deep darkness, on them has light shone. You have multiplied the nation; you have increased its joy; they rejoice before you as with joy at the harvest, as they are glad when they divide the spoil. For the yoke of his burden, and the staff for his shoulder, the rod of his oppressor, you have broken as on the day of Midian. For every boot of the tramping warrior in battle tumult and every garment rolled in blood will be burned as fuel for the fire.

This passage from Isaiah is probably most famous for verse 2a: "The people who walked in darkness have seen a great light." This offers a powerful image as we creep deeper into the long, dark hours of winter. The reality of the light of Christ entering into the darkness of our sinful, hopeless world has inspired countless carol lyrics, including "yonder breaks a new and glorious morn."

But there is a lesser-known verse from this same passage that has failed to affect hymn writers in the same way: "For every boot of the tramping warrior in battle tumult and every garment rolled in blood will be burned as fuel for the fire" (v. 5). Fa la la la la, la la la lahh! Tramping warriors, bullet-riddled battlefields, and garments rolled in blood aren't the kinds of props you can easily work into the church Christmas pageant. Such images rarely come to mind when we think of Advent. But maybe they should.

The theme of battle is dominant throughout these verses. The Israelites are captive to the darkness (v. 2). They rejoice like warriors dividing the plunder (v. 3). God's salvation will be like the day of Midian (v. 4), when he whittled Gideon's forces down to 300 troops before sending them (weaponless) to fight 135,000, ultimately working a miraculous victory.

Beneath the battle scars, Isaiah is painting a gospel masterpiece: God wins the victory, and we get the spoils! The Israelites did nothing to win the war. They didn't even fight. The Lord did. He overpowered their enemies, yet they still got their pick of the plunder.

This is precisely what Jesus does for us. He enters our world. He overpowers the strong man. He wins the battle. And he brings a divine ceasefire. It's only when every vestige of darkness has been eradicated that we can experience peace. **Jesus will allow no enemy to stand in between us and the Promised Land, our promised home.** A home where the spoils of battle are handed over freely to us: joy, peace, and hope.

Perhaps this year, instead of roasting chestnuts, we should burn a bloody boot to remind us that Jesus came as a conquering warrior-king to curb-stomp the forces of sin, death, and the devil once and for all–and that he's coming back soon to finish the job.

Lord,

THANK YOU FOR CONTINUALLY DEFEATING THE FORCES OF DARKNESS IN THIS LIFE THAT ARE TOO STRONG FOR ME TO MANAGE, AND FOR PROMISING ME A HOME WHERE THE SPOILS OF YOUR VICTORY ON THE CROSS WILL BE ETERNALLY MINE.

Amen.

A Glorious Resting Place

ISAIAH 11:10

In that day the root of Jesse, who shall stand as a signal for the peoples—of him shall the nations inquire, and his resting place shall be glorious.

The best nativity sets are the ones that aren't fancy, but handmade. The ones you couldn't get $10 for at a yard sale. The ones no one would call glorious, but are made of crude wire and plaster and chipped paint. These are the best because somehow they are an appropriate depiction of the first Advent of the root of Jesse (Jesus). It seems only angels and shepherds cared about the birth of Christ, the night it happened. There was the signal in the form of a star that a few men from the east took interest in, but other than that, the celestial signal was largely ignored by the world. And yet lying in a barn in Bethlehem was God wrapped in flesh. This resting place was not glorious, and the world did not inquire of him.

The second coming of the root of Jesse will be quite different. There will be no missing or ignoring it. Christ riding on the cloud will not be a signal you can dismiss. And the nations of the world will be called home to the place Jesus left to prepare for us. Not a home of mangers, but of heavenly mansions. A home without sin, death, or the devil. A home where all our strength and joy come from resting in the finished work of Jesus for us. The resting place of God is indeed glorious, and it is yours in Jesus Christ.

This year, as I look at the humble nativity at my grandmother's house, I will be reminded that Jesus came just as he said. That he has forgiven my sins and will come again to take me to the rest of his home. And it will be glorious indeed.

Heavenly Father,

HELP ME REST IN THE WORK OF CHRIST ON MY BEHALF, AND INCREASE MY HOPE IN HIS PROMISED RETURN.

Amen.

The Road Home

ISAIAH 35:1-10

The wilderness and the dry land shall be glad; the desert shall rejoice and blossom like the crocus; it shall blossom abundantly and rejoice with joy and singing. The glory of Lebanon shall be given to it, the majesty of Carmel and Sharon. They shall see the glory of the Lord, the majesty of our God. Strengthen the weak hands, and make firm the feeble knees. Say to those who have an anxious heart, "Be strong; fear not! Behold, your God will come with vengeance, with the recompense of God. He will come and save you." Then the eyes of the blind shall be opened, and the ears of the deaf unstopped; then shall the lame man leap like a deer, and the tongue of the mute sing for joy. For waters break forth in the wilderness, and streams in the desert; the burning sand shall become a pool, and the thirsty ground springs of water; in the haunt of jackals, where they lie down, the grass shall become reeds and rushes. And a highway shall be there, and it shall be called the Way of Holiness; the unclean shall not pass over it. It shall belong to those who walk on the way; even if they are fools, they shall not go astray. No lion shall be there, nor shall any ravenous beast come up on it; they shall not be found there, but the redeemed shall walk there. And the ransomed of the Lord shall return and come to Zion with singing; everlasting joy shall be upon their heads; they shall obtain gladness and joy, and sorrow and sighing shall flee away.

Sin and rebellion have cut off the Israelites - and all nations - from God, yet there is still hope; there is still a way home. Martin Luther argued that these verses lay out both grand and hidden promises for the church; for the church is truly home for all of God's people. Despite the surrounding deserts of the world, the church is where we find joy and singing. It's where God's glory is revealed to us through the preaching of the cross and where springs of forgiveness and righteousness burst forth from the sacraments.

Week after week, God's people gather in the wilderness to be fetched home via God's Way of Holiness. We have access to this road not through our own merits or accomplishments, but only through God's word which cleans us, renews us and keeps us from going astray – even if (and when) we are fools (v. 8).

Perhaps this Advent season you feel like the distance home is too far, too dangerous, too costly. You aren't prepared for the journey. Despite the holiday cheer, you have a fearful heart (v. 4) and worry that the highway is not for you. You fret that the front door into God's presence is locked. Yet Isaiah proclaims, "Be strong; fear not!" God has not only laid out the highway for you, he has also promised to come and save you. **In other words, God hasn't just made a way home, he is the way.** Christ has come. And he will come again so that the ransomed of the Lord - God's church - shall walk, free from all obstacles and enemies, straight into his embrace.

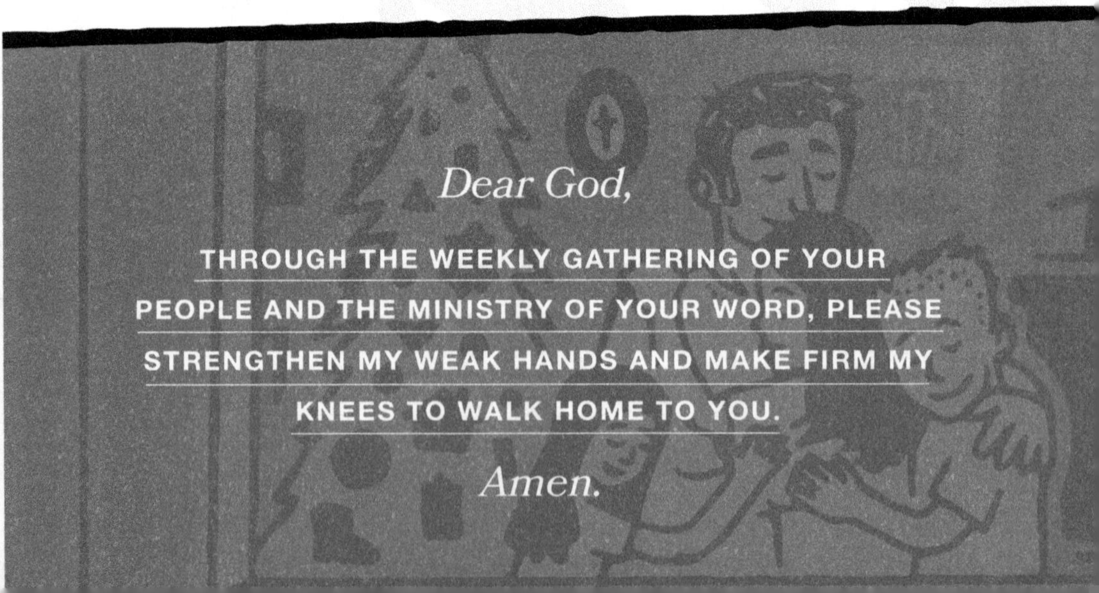

Dear God,

THROUGH THE WEEKLY GATHERING OF YOUR PEOPLE AND THE MINISTRY OF YOUR WORD, PLEASE STRENGTHEN MY WEAK HANDS AND MAKE FIRM MY KNEES TO WALK HOME TO YOU.

Amen.

The Comforts of Faith

ISAIAH 40:1-8

Comfort, comfort my people, says your God. Speak tenderly to Jerusalem, and cry to her that her warfare is ended, that her iniquity is pardoned, that she has received from the Lord's hand double for all her sins. A voice cries: "In the wilderness prepare the way of the Lord; make straight in the desert a highway for our God. Every valley shall be lifted up, and every mountain and hill be made low; the uneven ground shall become level, and the rough places a plain. And the glory of the Lord shall be revealed, and all flesh shall see it together, for the mouth of the Lord has spoken." A voice says, "Cry!" And I said, "What shall I cry?" All flesh is grass, and all its beauty is like the flower of the field. The grass withers, the flower fades when the breath of the Lord blows on it; surely the people are grass. The grass withers, the flower fades, but the word of our God will stand forever.

We often refer to "the comforts of home," when we are weary, homesick, or navigating life's trials. Home is where we are most ourselves - where we rest, dwell with those who know and love us, and create cherished memories. In times of suffering, what we wouldn't give for the comforts of home.

The Protestant Reformers referred to faith in a similar way. They believed faith in God's promises (fulfilled through Christ) "comforts the terrified mind and brings it peace."[1] Just as we return home - at the end of a long day or during the holidays - Christians return to God's promises as our consolation from sin, death, and the devil.

This is why in Isaiah 40, when the prophet opens the second half of his book "dancing with promises,"[2] as Martin Luther says, he first sets the stage with nothing other than comfort itself. Comfort which springs forth from peace, forgiveness, and God's unreasonable grace (v. 2). What greater consolation to the terrors of our consciences than the unbelievable promise that through Christ, we receive *double* for all our sins.

You might know a bit of what this is like if you consider how your mom, despite slaving away all day to cook a Christmas feast (which you didn't help with at all), gives you a double portion of your favorite side dish. Or despite that large fight you had about putting together the kids Christmas toys, your spouse stays up twice as long as you on Christmas Eve to make sure everything is ready.

Just like these comforts of home, God's promises defy our understanding and yet he still gives them in abundance through Christ. **His gospel is our comfort, and therefore it is our home.**

[1] Philip Melanchthon and Charles Leander Hill, *The Loci communes of Philip Melanchthon*, trans. Charles Leander Hill (Boston: Meador, 1944), 154.

[2] Martin Luther, *Luther's Works*, Vol. 17: Lectures on Isaiah: Chapters 40-66, ed. Jaroslav Jan Pelikan, Hilton C. Oswald, and Helmut T. Lehmann, vol. 17 (Saint Louis, MO: Concordia Publishing House, 1999), 3.

He Won't and He Will

ISAIAH 9:1-5

Behold my servant, whom I uphold, my chosen, in whom my soul delights; I have put my Spirit upon him; he will bring forth justice to the nations. He will not cry aloud or lift up his voice, or make it heard in the street; a bruised reed he will not break, and a faintly burning wick he will not quench; he will faithfully bring forth justice. He will not grow faint or be discouraged till he has established justice in the earth; and the coastlands wait for his law. Thus says God, the Lord, who created the heavens and stretched them out, who spread out the earth and what comes from it, who gives breath to the people on it and spirit to those who walk in it:

"I am the Lord; I have called you in righteousness; I will take you by the hand and keep you; I will give you

as a covenant for the people, a light for the nations, to open the eyes that are blind, to bring out the prisoners from the dungeon, from the prison those who sit in darkness. I am the Lord; that is my name; my glory I give to no other, nor my praise to carved idols. Behold, the former things have come to pass, and new things I now declare; before they spring forth I tell you of them."

The Holy Spirit directs Isaiah to preach that the arrival of God's Servant will be nothing but good news. And, boy, did the people of Judah need some good news. Because of their sin, they were exiled and far from home. Just like you and me, they were suffocating under their guilt and shame. Just like you and me, they know what it's like to be crushed by the law on account of sin, to feel like we are about to break, to feel like the light of our faith is about to go out.

So Isaiah preaches to us the good news of the Servant of the Lord, to reconcile with us and to bring us home. He tells us that there are things the Servant will *not* do and there are things he *will* do.

This Servant will come in the power of that Holy Spirit, and he will not "cry aloud or lift up his voice" in judgement or terror towards those already in fear. For those bruised by their sin and at the breaking point "he will not break" them. He will not snuff out those "faintly burning wicks." This Servant is not interested in furthering punishment and judgment, but rather, in restoring righteousness. And, he will not "grow faint or be discouraged" until he has made all things right.

God *will* send his Servant in the power of the Spirit to those suffering, guilty, lost sinners who need righteousness. He *will* "open the eyes of the blind...bring out the prisoners from the dungeon." He *will* bring light into the darkness. He *will* do this by forgiving sins and declaring us righteous. He *will* bring about this forgiveness by dying in their place on a cross. In this way, he *will* "bring forth justice to the nations" by paying for their injustices with his blood. In this restored righteousness, he *will* "take you by the hand" and lead you home.

This is our Servant, Christ Jesus, the Righteous One, who *will* and *has* done this for you!

Almighty Father,

BECAUSE OF YOUR SON'S GREAT LOVE FOR US, YOU WILL NOT LEAVE US NOR FORSAKE US, BUT YOU WILL DRAW US HOME TO YOU. KEEP US EVER FAITHFUL.

Amen.

Created for Salvation

ISAIAH 43:1-3A

But now thus says the Lord, he who created you, O Jacob, he who formed you, O Israel: "Fear not, for I have redeemed you; I have called you by name, you are mine. When you pass through the waters, I will be with you; and through the rivers, they shall not overwhelm you; when you walk through fire you shall not be burned, and the flame shall not consume you. For I am the Lord your God, the Holy One of Israel, your Savior."

Fear God and don't be afraid are two of the most common refrains in Scripture. Which is it? Does God want you to fear him, or does he want to take away your fear? The answer is God wants us, who are burdened with so many fears, to fear him alone, so that he may take even that final fear away.

Notice what Isaiah says between the words "Now thus says the Lord" and "Fear not." It's not just any God speaking to you. It's the God who created you. The God who formed you. This means you are not an accident; you were deliberate. To be made on purpose is to be made with purpose. That purpose is to belong to God.

The truth is, we are all runaways that God has pursued in Christ. **The incarnation is God refusing to let what he has created live apart from him.** It is God running to the runaway. He has called us by name and declared that despite all our running, we belong to him. God looks at every rebellious child and says, "mine." The God who walks on water says, "Fear not the river, I will be with you." The God who has conquered Hell says, "Fear not the flame, I am your Savior."

God has wanted you from the beginning. You were created and formed for salvation, not fear. To be saved by God is to be rescued from sin, death, the devil, and fear. To be redeemed is to be brought back to the home our first parents ran away from so long ago, and to discover we always belonged with God.

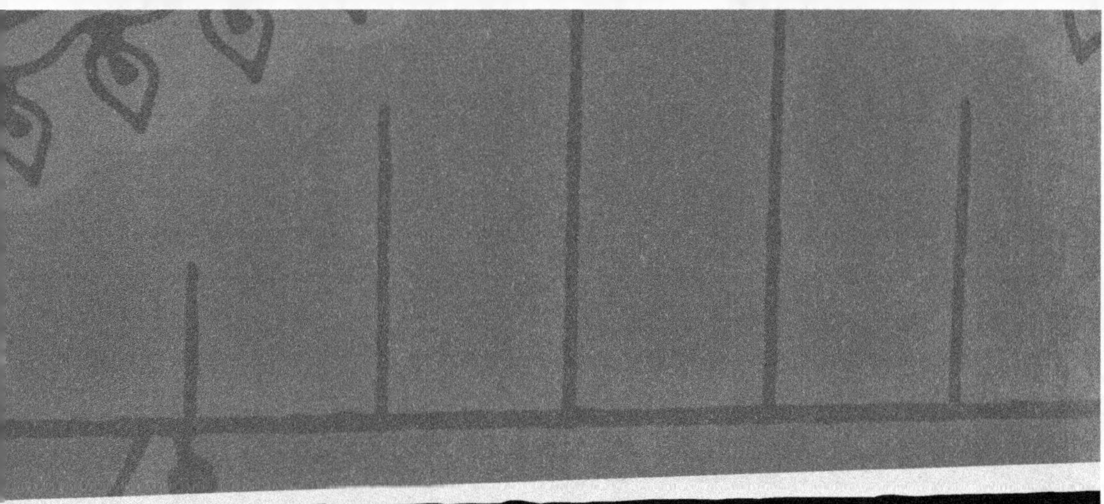

Heavenly Father,

ROOT MY IDENTITY IN BELONGING TO YOU AND QUICKLY PURSUE ME WHEN I WANDER AWAY.

Amen.

Your God Reigns

ISAIAH 52:7-10

How beautiful upon the mountains are the feet of him who brings good news, who publishes peace, who brings good news of happiness, who publishes salvation, who says to Zion, "Your God reigns." The voice of your watchmen—they lift up their voice; together they sing for joy; for eye to eye they see the return of the Lord to Zion. Break forth together into singing, you waste places of Jerusalem, for the Lord has comforted his people; he has redeemed Jerusalem. The Lord has bared his holy arm before the eyes of all the nations, and all the ends of the earth shall see the salvation of our God.

The word "gospel" or Good News comes from the Greek *euangelion*. The Hebrew equivalent is the verb *basar*, which also means "to bring news," but with a distinctly military flavor. In ancient Israel, to *basar* was to run from the battlefield with a cry of victory.

That is what's happening in Isaiah 52:7, "How beautiful upon the mountains are the feet of him who brings good news [*basar*], who publishes peace, who brings good news [*basar*] of happiness, who publishes salvation, who says to Zion, 'Your God reigns.'"

This message is not abstract or philosophical—it is the joyful shout of a herald who announces that God has bared his holy arm, defeated his enemies, reclaimed his people.

The incarnation is where it all begins. **God lands on enemy territory inside a virgin's womb.** He might not look like a Warrior King, wrapped in those swaddling clothes, but the Lord often shows up on our doorstep in seemingly unlordly ways.

Violence pursues him as murderous Herod wants him dead. His townspeople try to throw him from a cliff. Plotters plot, schemers scheme, and "the nations rage and the peoples plot in vain against him" (Ps. 2:1).

But this is what he signed up for. He came to fight for us, and to protect us from the enemies which surround us, threatening to knock down our doors, and the enemies within that tempt to consume us, house and home. No longer wrapped in swaddling clothes but in a burial shroud, this Warrior King, having soaked up all sin and death and hate on the battlefield of the cross, finished the job.

And we? Rescued by him from the domain of darkness, brought from death to life in his love, we break forth into singing, for we have seen the salvation of our God, Jesus the Christ, and we raise our voices in harmony as we find ourselves safe at home on Mount Zion, looking in hope for his return.

How beautiful are the feet of the herald who brings the good news that the one in the manger, who hung on the cross, has exited the tomb and now reigns over us as our merciful King.

King Jesus,

OUR WARRIOR AND REDEEMER, GUARD US AND GUIDE US AS WE ENJOY THE FREEDOM OF LIFE IN YOUR EVERLASTING KINGDOM.

Amen.

Sheep Gone Astray

ISAIAH 53:4-6

Surely he has borne our griefs and carried our sorrows; yet we esteemed him stricken, smitten by God, and afflicted. But he was pierced for our transgressions; he was crushed for our iniquities; upon him was the chastisement that brought us peace, and with his wounds we are healed. All we like sheep have gone astray; we have turned—every one—to his own way; and the Lord has laid on him the iniquity of us all.

At the very end of Psalm 119, having rejoiced for 175 verses in the Word of God, we make this humbling confession, "I have gone astray like a lost sheep; seek your servant" (v. 119:176).

How fitting is that? If there's ever a time when it seems we should not be going astray, it's when we have been walking on the Lord's long highway of Psalm 119. Yet even then, we lose our way. We mortals are like that: wayward and weak, wandering off to graze on poisonous weeds when our Shepherd has made us lie down in green pastures.

So Isaiah says, "All we like sheep have gone astray; we have turned—every one—to his own way" (v. 6). Every sheep does what is right in his own eyes. One is surrounded by wolves. Another teeters on a cliff edge. Still another is bogged down in mud.

That is why the Servant of Isaiah 53 does not show up to lend us a hand, to give us some sound advice on how to kick-start our self-salvation. He doesn't even ask us if we want to be saved. He just does it.

For all of us lost sheep, homeless in our own ways, our Good Shepherd becomes the Lamb of God who takes away the sin of the world. Our griefs, he bears. Our sorrows, he carries. For our transgressions and iniquities, he is pierced and crushed. In taking our sin away, he restores us to the safety of his flock and brings us home.

Jesus, from cradle to grave, was soaking up the sickness, suffering, and sin of the world. His entire life was a saving swap. He takes our bad and gives us his good, that we might forever be the lambs of his flock and the sheep of his pasture.

Good Shepherd,

FIND US, CARRY US HOME, AND ALWAYS KEEP US CLOSE TO YOU, FOR IN YOUR WOUNDS WE ARE HEALED.

Amen.

You Can't Buy What is Already Free

ISAIAH 55:1-5

Come, everyone who thirsts, come to the waters; and he who has no money, come, buy and eat! Come, buy wine and milk without money and without price. Why do you spend your money for that which is not bread, and your labor for that which does not satisfy? Listen diligently to me, and eat what is good, and delight yourselves in rich food. Incline your ear, and come to me; hear, that your soul may live; and I will make with you an everlasting covenant, my steadfast, sure love for David. Behold, I made him a witness to the peoples, a leader and commander for the peoples. Behold, you shall call a nation that you do not know, and a nation that did not know you shall run to you, because of the Lord your God, and of the Holy One of Israel, for he has glorified you.

Parties, feasts, and neverending gifts fill our calendars and our homes this time of year. Yet, ironically, the outward excess of the holiday season sometimes only serves to reinforce our loneliness and homesickness. And even when our festivities offer joy, good company and belonging, and filling food, once all the trimmings come down, the leftovers have been tossed, and silence again fills our rooms, we are confronted with the truth that, here and now, even the merriest of homes isn't permanent, and our food and drink never fully satisfy.

In chapter 55, the prophet Isaiah offers us a feast greater than anything the holiday season could conjure up. From the very first verse, we know this is a different type of gathering because everyone who thirsts (which is to say every man, woman, and child) is invited. We are invited "to buy" but without money and without price.

Even our most lavish attempts at generosity can't produce gifts like this. The human heart runs on expectation and quantification. We accept gifts, only to feel guilty later that we didn't remember to give something in return. We adore spoiling our loved ones, but later our feelings get hurt when they don't act as grateful as we would hope. We refuse to accept anything as truly free but instead prefer to work for what Isaiah says does not satisfy: whether that's holiday festivities or the works we assume will lead us to righteousness.

And yet, the gifts of the Lord are impossible to buy. There is absolutely *nothing* we can give in order to receive God's gifts; laboring for them will do you no good (and may even ruin them). His invitation to dwell with him is only as good as it is free. The bread of his word is so rich that it fills both our stomachs and our souls. And we eat it not through our mouths, but through our ears.

These are the strange and wonderful truths of God's feast, which never ends when we find ourselves in his presence. Whether you find yourself joyful or forlorn this Advent season, at home or far from it, **remember that you are called now and forevermore to enter God's home and partake at his table**; so fill your ears with his word, and delight in the food and drink of his salvation and righteousness.

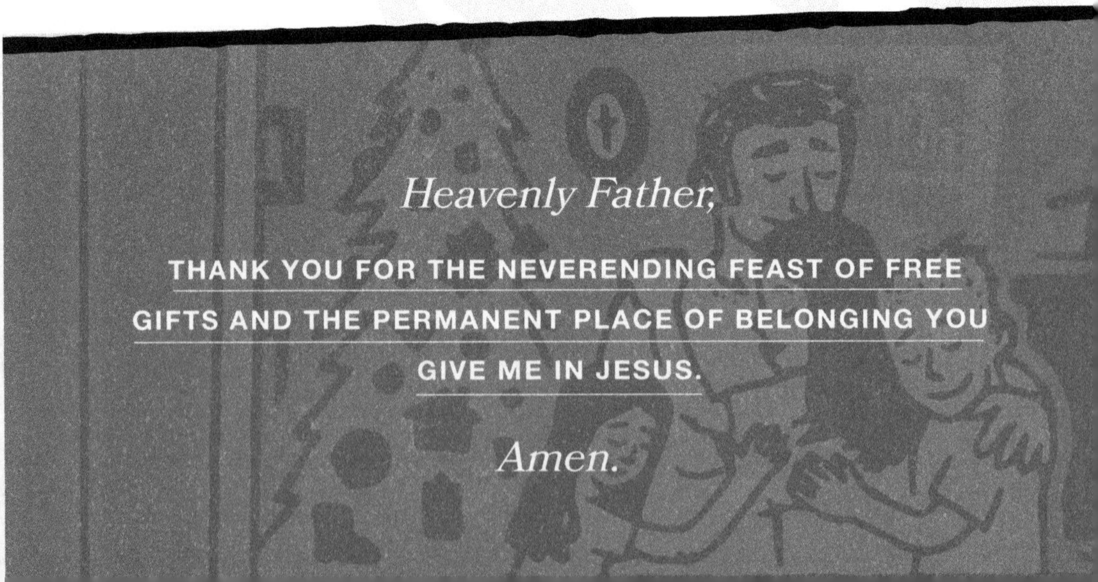

Heavenly Father,

THANK YOU FOR THE NEVERENDING FEAST OF FREE GIFTS AND THE PERMANENT PLACE OF BELONGING YOU GIVE ME IN JESUS.

Amen.

You Don't Have to Tell Me Twice

ISAIAH 60:1-3

Arise, shine, for your light has come, and the glory of the Lord has risen upon you. For behold, darkness shall cover the earth, and thick darkness the peoples; but the Lord will arise upon you, and his glory will be seen upon you. And nations shall come to your light, and kings to the brightness of your rising.

There are some commands that cause us to rejoice. Every kid on Christmas morning knows what I am talking about. No child hears, "Wake up!" without flying out of bed to get to the tree. That command lands more like an announcement of good things to come! Or, think about going on a trip to Disneyland. When Dad says, "Get in the car," it's not a demand one hears and thinks, "Disneyland depends upon my willingness to sincerely obey my dad." Rather, this is a command with a promise attached to it: "Disneyland awaits!" The response is not the sinful "Do I have to?" but the gospel-induced "You don't have to tell me twice!"

Such is the language of Isaiah for those long dead in their sins and trespasses. "Arise, shine, for your light has come, and the glory of the LORD has risen upon you" (v. 1). This is Jesus calling guilty, greedy Zaccheaus out of the tree, "Zaccheaus, hurry and come down, for I must stay at your house today!" (Luke 19:5) This is the resurrection call of Jesus to Lazarus after four smelly days in the tomb, "Lazarus, come out!" (John 11:43) This is the language of the Lord's Supper when Jesus is about to put his forgiving, life-giving body and blood in your open mouth, "Take and eat...take and drink..." Is there any sinner, dead in their guilt, who knows their need that must hear that a second time?

So it is that Jesus speaks to you who live in the darkness of sin and in the cruel thick darkness that covers the earth. And it is Jesus who is calling you to come and dwell in his presence, a place filled with his bright peace. **Christ has risen from the dead and conquered the darkness for you, so you may come, like the nations, to his light.** So, hear this! Christmas morning is here, the tomb is empty, Christ has risen for you! Arise? Shine? You don't have to tell me twice!

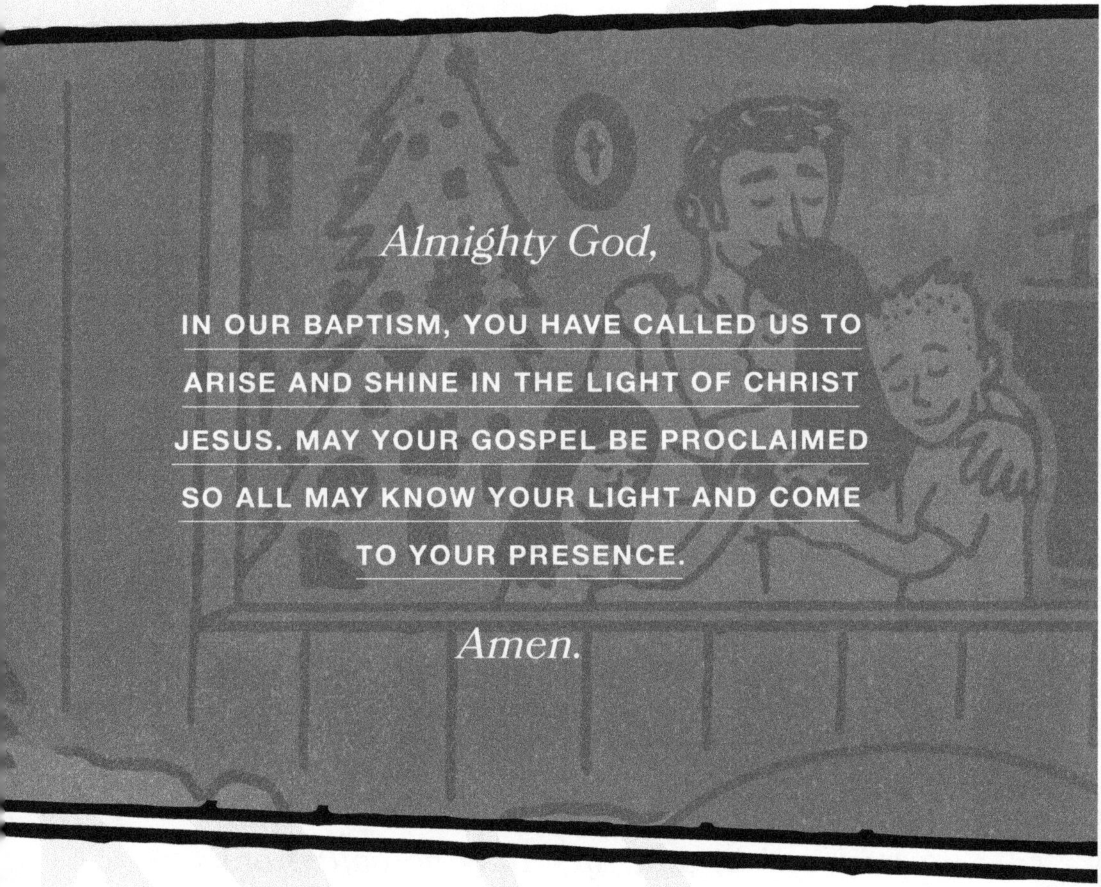

Almighty God,

IN OUR BAPTISM, YOU HAVE CALLED US TO ARISE AND SHINE IN THE LIGHT OF CHRIST JESUS. MAY YOUR GOSPEL BE PROCLAIMED SO ALL MAY KNOW YOUR LIGHT AND COME TO YOUR PRESENCE.

Amen.

Anointed to Unlock Cells

ISAIAH 61:1-3

"The Spirit of the Lord God is upon me, because the Lord has anointed me to bring good news to the poor; he has sent me to bind up the brokenhearted, to proclaim liberty to the captives, and the opening of the prison to those who are bound; to proclaim the year of the Lord's favor, and the day of vengeance of our God; to comfort all who mourn; to grant to those who mourn in Zion—to give them a beautiful headdress instead of ashes, the oil of gladness instead of mourning, the garment of praise instead of a faint spirit; that they may be called oaks of righteousness, the planting of the Lord, that he may be glorified."

An old preacher once said, “Good sermons sound like cell doors being unlocked.” It seems likely that he pulled that from Isaiah 61. This chapter of Isaiah was also the text for Jesus’ first sermon. A sermon that was short and shocking. He simply read the text and said, “Today this Scripture has been fulfilled in your hearing” (Luke 4:21). What glorious news for us! **Jesus is the fulfillment of Isaiah 61.** The Lord has anointed him for the purpose of bringing good news to poor, brokenhearted captives like us.

We are the spiritually poor. We are bankrupt of all righteousness. And yet there is Jesus making us rich in his righteousness. Preaching the good news that in him we have more than we could hope for. We are the brokenhearted. We live lives scarred in suffering and loss. We carry shame, regret, and grief. And yet there is Jesus, taking all of that into himself, comforting us with his love and gifting us his peace. We are the captives. Locked away in the prison of sin with no hope of returning home. And yet, there is Jesus unlocking every cell door and breaking every chain with the power of his death and resurrection. This is the work Jesus has been anointed to do. He left his heavenly home to preach the good news of forgiveness, freedom, and eternal life to the helpless, hopeless, and homeless.

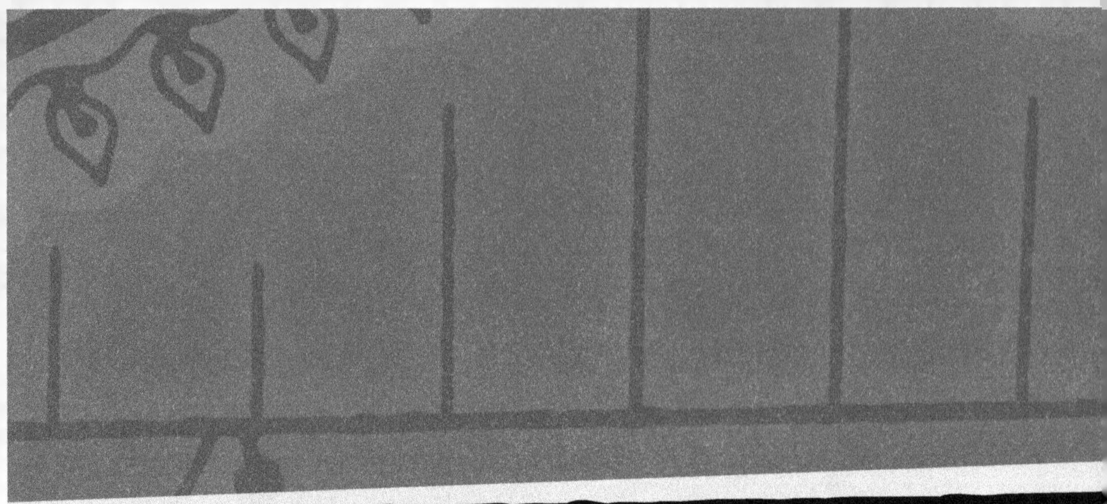

Heavenly Father,

THANK YOU FOR SENDING YOUR SON TO UNLOCK MY PRISON DOORS, AND FOR GIVING ME THE GOOD NEWS THAT I AM FORGIVEN AND I WILL ONE DAY RETURN TO MY ETERNAL HOME.

Amen.

A Wedding to Remember

ISAIAH 62:1-5

For Zion's sake I will not keep silent, and for Jerusalem's sake I will not be quiet, until her righteousness goes forth as brightness, and her salvation as a burning torch. The nations shall see your righteousness, and all the kings your glory, and you shall be called by a new name that the mouth of the Lord will give. You shall be a crown of beauty in the hand of the Lord, and a royal diadem in the hand of your God. You shall no more be termed Forsaken, and your land shall no more be termed Desolate, but you shall be called My Delight Is in Her, and your land Married; for the Lord delights in you, and your land shall be married. For as a young man marries a young woman, so shall your sons marry you, and as the bridegroom rejoices over the bride, so shall your God rejoice over you.

Weddings are a big deal. From picking the venue to choosing the dress to narrowing down the guest list to hiring the DJ, the excitement of a wedding builds with each step until finally, the big day arrives. The guests are seated. The bridesmaids and groomsmen process. All eyes shift to the back of the sanctuary. The music changes. The doors open. The congregation rises. And the bride appears in all of her finery, making her way down the aisle toward her expectant groom, who stands at the altar grinning from ear-to-ear.

This passage from Isaiah centers on a wedding, but there are some unique features of this particular ceremony, including God's promise to change the land of Israel from "Desolate" to "Married." The bride (Israel) will be renamed by her bridegroom (the Lord); her fortunes reversed and transformed. Israel had sinned greatly by chasing after the false gods of the surrounding nations, and the consequences were severe. The Babylonians had invaded and ravaged the promised land, the Temple was destroyed, their homes were burned, and all hope for the future went up in smoke. In the midst of this devastation, however, the Lord was actually planning a wedding. He would cleanse and restore her, put a ring on her finger, and give her his own name. Ultimately, he would change this dusty ghost town into a verdant wedding venue, overflowing with wine and guests.

Are you in a desolate place right now? Do you feel less like a pure spotless bride and more like an unwanted guest at your own wedding? Fear not, because the love of your groom is unconditional! He is not embarrassed by your brokenness or failures or past. **Like a groom at the altar, he delights in you. He can't take his eyes off of you.** He embraces you. When God lifts the veil on his bride, he too is grinning from ear-to-ear, because he doesn't see a stained wedding dress but only the seamless, spotless garment of the perfect Lamb of God. For those in Christ, he never hesitates to pick us up, carry us across the threshold, and bring us back home.

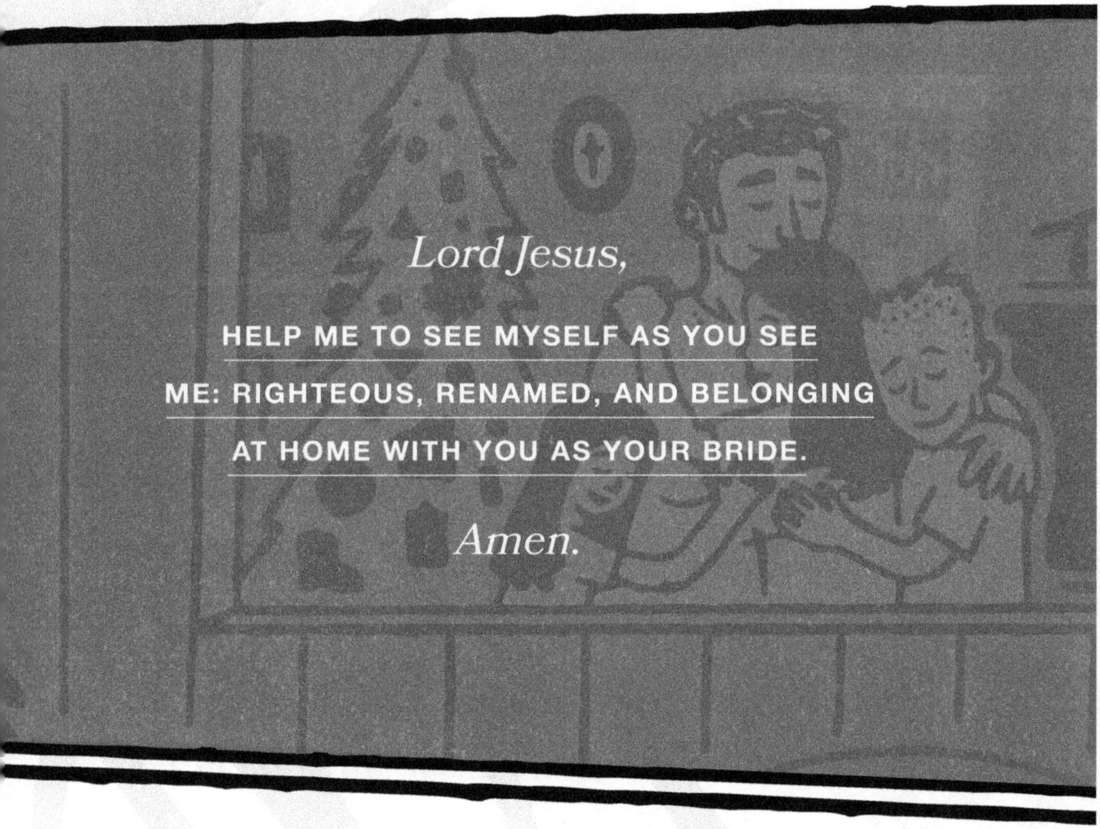

Lord Jesus,

HELP ME TO SEE MYSELF AS YOU SEE ME: RIGHTEOUS, RENAMED, AND BELONGING AT HOME WITH YOU AS YOUR BRIDE.

Amen.

Remember Forever

ISAIAH 63:7-9

I will recount the steadfast love of the Lord, the praises of the Lord, according to all that the Lord has granted us, and the great goodness to the house of Israel that he has granted them according to his compassion, according to the abundance of his steadfast love. For he said, "Surely they are my people, children who will not deal falsely." And he became their Savior. In all their affliction he was afflicted, and the angel of his presence saved them; in his love and in his pity he redeemed them; he lifted them up and carried them all the days of old.

"You make sure that they remember–FOREVER–the night they played the Titans!" Coach Yoast delivers these words during an iconic scene in Disney's *Remember the Titans*, rallying his beleaguered football team to action. He knew something they didn't: On the gridiron, only action would solidify their memory in the collective imagination of T.C. Williams High School, causing others to tell of their deeds.

Isaiah knew something similar, because God's actions on behalf of Israel were seared into his memory. For Isaiah, God's "steadfast love" wasn't just an idea or an abstract philosophical concept. It didn't exist out in the ether but down in the dirt; in literal blood, sweat, and tears–in the blood of passover lambs and in the waters of the Red Sea and in the bonded hydrogen and oxygen molecules that flowed out at Meribah. God didn't simply *say* he loved his people. He *showed* it, again and again through his deeds. Perhaps most especially, even through their suffering.

God identifies with the suffering of his people, even if that suffering is self-inflicted. Here in Isaiah, the Israelites were in the midst of some pretty terrible pain, experiencing God's judgment against their idolatrous ways as they languished in exile. But God refused to allow their faithlessness to stand in the way of his solidarity with them: "In all their distress, he too was distressed, and the angel of his presence saved them" (v. 9). Self-inflicted or not, God's fidelity toward his people would not waver. He showed compassion, brought them to repentance, and forgave all of their sins. God would not allow his people to remain spiritually homeless but would instead return them from exile and give them a place to belong. In other words, God never took down the "Welcome Home!" banner.

But God went one step further. Despite the fact that the Israelites had a checkered past and had shown themselves to be hard-hearted over and over, God says something astounding: "Surely they are my people, *children who will not deal falsely*" (v. 8). Like a merciful parent who trusts their child even after he or she has just broken a window–effectively proving themselves untrustworthy–**our Heavenly Father imputes pure motives to us**. How can he do such a thing? Only by looking at us through the lens of the Lamb. God's love makes possible such a secure home–a household where that trust can grow, relationships can flourish, and we can be given a place to belong.

Truly, that is a deed worth remembering–forever.

Heavenly Father,

THANK YOU FOR REDEEMING ME FROM THE EXILE OF SIN. CONTINUE TO LIFT ME UP, AND CARRY ME ALL THE DAYS OF MY LIFE UNTIL I COME TO DWELL IN YOUR HOUSE.

Amen.

God Comes for Sinners

ISAIAH 64:1-9

Oh that you would rend the heavens and come down, that the mountains might quake at your presence—as when fire kindles brushwood and the fire causes water to boil—to make your name known to your adversaries, and that the nations might tremble at your presence! When you did awesome things that we did not look for, you came down, the mountains quaked at your presence. From of old no one has heard or perceived by the ear, no eye has seen a God besides you, who acts for those who wait for him. You meet him who joyfully works righteousness, those who remember you in your ways. Behold, you were angry, and we sinned; in our sins we have been a long time, and shall we be saved? We have all become like one who is unclean, and all our righteous deeds are like a polluted garment. We all fade like a leaf, and our iniquities, like the wind, take us away. There is no one who calls upon your name, who rouses himself to take hold of you; for you have hidden your face from us, and have made us melt in the hand of our iniquities. But now, O Lord, you are our Father; we are the clay, and you are our potter; we are all the work of your hand. Be not so terribly angry, O Lord, and remember not iniquity forever. Behold, please look, we are all your people.

Be careful what you ask for from Santa. You know his naughty and nice list game, don't you? Those who do good make the "Nice" list and get presents and the warm embrace of home on Christmas morning. Those who break the rules end up on the "Naughty" list, rewarded only with coal, a clear admonishment that their behavior means they don't belong. We all want to be on the nice list—and, if we're honest, it feels satisfying when the naughty get what they deserve.

In Isaiah 64, we find Isaiah praying for justice to come upon the enemies of God's people and, thus, the enemies of God. He prays for God to make the nations tremble. After all, that is what God does to those who violate his law and sin against him. Let the naughty list justice come!

Isaiah reminds us that God favors “those who wait for him” and meets with those who “joyfully work righteousness” (vv. 4–5). But then comes a painful realization: “You were angry, and we sinned. In our sins we have been a long time, and shall we be saved?” (v. 5).

Isaiah wanted judgment for the wicked—until he remembered his own place before a holy God. Suddenly, the justice he prayed for seems terrifying. We too are sinners. We too belong on that naughty list. We too are outsiders looking in when it comes to righteousness. So Isaiah confesses sin and cries out for mercy. Will God listen?

These Advent cries are met with the good news of Christmas morning. The gift of Immanuel- God with us-means God has heard the pleas of his people in verse 9. **In Christ, he rends the heavens and comes down to tear up the naughty list.** Jesus, the one who “joyfully works righteousness,” took the record of sins that stood against you and nailed it to the cross (Col. 2:14). Because of him, you are assured a place forever on the nice list and a seat in front of the Christmas tree, surrounded by his good gifts. You wake up on Christmas morning, and every morning after, in the loving embrace of Christ. For in him, there is no condemnation left for you (Rom. 8:1).

Almighty God,

YOU LOOK UPON THE RIGHTEOUSNESS OF YOUR SON AND FREELY GIFT IT TO ME SO THAT I HAVE A PLACE IN YOUR HOME FOREVER. FORGIVE MY SINS AND LET THEM NEVER BE ADDED TO MY ACCOUNT FOR CHRIST'S SAKE.

Amen.

No More Tears for Christmas

ISAIAH 65:17-19

"For behold, I create new heavens and a new earth, and the former things shall not be remembered or come into mind. But be glad and rejoice forever in that which I create; for behold, I create Jerusalem to be a joy, and her people to be a gladness. I will rejoice in Jerusalem and be glad in my people; no more shall be heard in it the sound of weeping and the cry of distress...says the Lord."

What's wrong with tears? Tears induced by love don't seem all that bad. But, we know all too well, not all tears come from a place of love. Many tears come from the worst this world has to give: we weep over our sins, we are distressed over futures that seem hopeless. We've experienced the painful feeling that comes when separated from a loved one through death. What is more, many of us know what it means to live in a home filled with tears and pain. Guilt. Shame. Fear. Death. Weeping tarries while such enemies loom over our lives.

So, what if I told you that for Christmas, God has decided to give you the gift of removing your tears? This is why Jesus has come; this is the promise from Isaiah today. Jesus comes to take away the former things: your sinful past, the horrible reign of death, the tyranny of fear. All removed and replaced with the "new creation" presents of eternal gladness and rejoicing! All of these punishments from God that result from sin will turn to his joy and gladness in his people! With him present among us "no more shall be heard…the sound of weeping and the cry of distress!" (v. 19)

Jesus has come to remove all tears. As the Psalmist says, "Weeping may tarry for the night, but joy comes with the morning" (Ps. 30:5). **At the birth of Jesus, the morning is beginning**

to dawn. At his resurrection, our tears are beginning to dry. At that time, we will be welcomed into a home that is free from the tears of death, sorrow, fighting, and pain. A new heavens and a new earth, free from sin-induced tears. When he comes again, our sorrow will retreat, and we will rest easy: forever and eternally at home. Now, I bet many of us will weep for joy, and even then, with delight in his eyes, he will wipe away our tears and welcome us into his warm embrace.

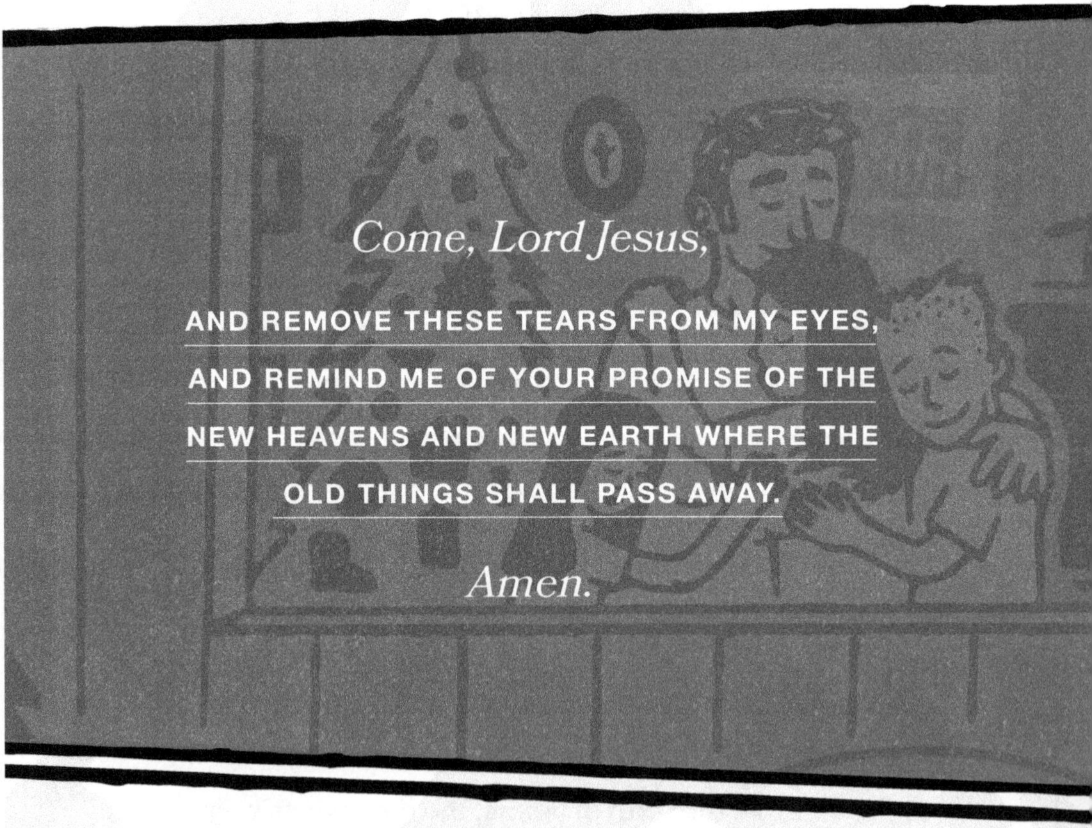

Come, Lord Jesus,

AND REMOVE THESE TEARS FROM MY EYES, AND REMIND ME OF YOUR PROMISE OF THE NEW HEAVENS AND NEW EARTH WHERE THE OLD THINGS SHALL PASS AWAY.

Amen.

The Gathering of God

ISAIAH 66:22-23

"For as the new heavens and the new earth that I make shall remain before me, says the Lord, so shall your offspring and your name remain. From new moon to new moon, and from Sabbath to Sabbath, all flesh shall come to worship before me, declares the Lord."

The best part about the holidays is the gathering of family and friends. Eating and drinking together. Sharing and making memories. The older we get, the more faces there are missing from those gatherings. In between Christmas mornings, there are gatherings at bedsides and funeral homes. Death has a way of making those living feel helpless. Grief and its effects are real. And yet, it's also good to remember we shouldn't give death back the power that Jesus has stripped from it. **Jesus has defeated death and made it his servant.** It is now a vehicle God uses to gather his people home.

The promise in Isaiah 66 is about that home after death. It's the promise that God will make a new heavens and a new earth for you to dwell in. A new home free from suffering and sin. There you will see the glory of God. This glory is a person: God made flesh in Jesus Christ. And you will not be alone. You will join in the great gathering of brothers and sisters from every time, tongue, and nation. The holy reunion with those you love and the family you never knew you had. No faces will ever be missing, and the joy will never cease as you revel in the truth that on Christmas, God declared war on death for you, and on Easter, he declared his victory.

Heavenly Father,

THANK YOU FOR THE PROMISE THAT YOU WILL GATHER YOUR CHILDREN TO BE WITH YOU AND MAKE ALL OUR GATHERINGS UNTIL THEN REMINDERS OF THAT GREAT GATHERING TO COME.

Amen.

Let Us Reason Together

ISAIAH 1:18-20

Come now, let us reason together, says the Lord: though your sins are like scarlet, they shall be as white as snow; though they are red like crimson, they shall become like wool. If you are willing and obedient, you shall eat the good of the land; but if you refuse and rebel, you shall be eaten by the sword; for the mouth of the Lord has spoken.

"Come now, let us reason together, says the Lord," (v. 18). Have a seat, my child, our Father seems to be saying to us. My, oh, my. You have, like a lost sheep, wandered far away and gotten yourself into many troubles. Dirtied with the mud of a hundred different puddles of vice. Blooded by the fangs of demonic wolves. You are far away from home.

You have, like the prodigal, gone off into a faraway country, lost everything, and fouled yourself with the slop of pigs. From the sole of your foot to the crown of your head, there is not a single clean spot. You're a sight to behold, and not a pretty one.

"Come now, let us reason together, says the Lord." Let's think this through. There's certainly nothing that you can do to wipe off the filth. You would just smear it further. There is nothing for you in you.

But there is something I can and will do, says the Lord. "Though your sins are like scarlet, they shall be as white as snow; though they are red like crimson, they shall become like wool" (v. 18).

"But how?" we ask. We are too deeply stained. We are too far gone.

But the God of mercy does not acknowledge our "too's." There is no "too much" for him.

He does not say, "Though your sins are like scarlet, they shall be as a dusty rose; though they are red like crimson, they shall become gray as a dove." He is the Lord of extremes: from death to life, from darkness to light, from scarlet to snow, from crimson to wool.

"Halfway" or "good enough" is not in his vocabulary. He is the God of "It is finished."

And by finished, he means precisely that: Done. Complete. **In the divine detergent of the blood of the Lamb, he has washed and purified us.** In Christ we are a sight to behold, and a pretty one. Beautiful in his eyes. We are wool-white sheep who follow the voice of our Good Shepherd, to eat the good of the land. We are sons and daughters of the Father, once exiled and far away, but now brought lovingly back into his household, a host of saints arrayed in white.

Come now, O Lord,

AND WASH US, CLOTHE US, AND DO FOR US IN MERCY WHAT WE COULD NEVER DO FOR OURSELVES: KEEP US AS YOUR SONS AND DAUGHTERS.

Amen.

Beautiful and Glorious

ISAIAH 4:2-6

In that day the branch of the Lord shall be beautiful and glorious, and the fruit of the land shall be the pride and honor of the survivors of Israel. And he who is left in Zion and remains in Jerusalem will be called holy, everyone who has been recorded for life in Jerusalem, when the Lord shall have washed away the filth of the daughters of Zion and cleansed the bloodstains of Jerusalem from its midst by a spirit of judgment and by a spirit of burning. Then the Lord will create over the whole site of Mount Zion and over her assemblies a cloud by day, and smoke and the shining of a flaming fire by night; for over all the glory there will be a canopy. There will be a booth for shade by day from the heat, and for a refuge and a shelter from the storm and rain.

"In that day the branch of the Lord shall be beautiful and glorious" (v. 2). This "branch" is a title for the Messiah in the Old Testament, the one who branches forth from the stump of Jesse to become the new and better Tree of Life, beautiful in mercy, glorious in power.

He gathers us to himself and makes us holy by his Holy Spirit, everyone who has been recorded for life in Jerusalem. He has inked your name indelibly in the Book of Life, written in the red of his sacrificial blood, marking you as a citizen of his kingdom, a temple of his Spirit, a member of the body of Christ.

The Lord has washed away the filth of the daughters of Zion and cleansed the bloodstains of Jerusalem. In the flood of forgiveness that flowed from the pierced side of our crucified Savior, all the filth of our sin is gone, all the bloodstains of iniquity purged. He has baptized us with the Holy Spirit and fire, burning away the dross of death and filling us with the fire of his love.

As he did for Israel in the wilderness, guiding and sheltering them with a pillar of cloud and fire until he brought them to their new home in the land of promise, so he does for us. **He brings us to our new home in him, the fulfillment of all**

God's promises. Then the Lord has created over the whole site of Mount Zion and over her assemblies a cloud by day, and smoke and the shining of a flaming fire by night. We are shaded, sheltered, and shielded by our Immanuel, God with us.

And over all the glory there will be a canopy—a wedding canopy, for the Son of God makes us his bride, resplendent in his righteousness, betrothed to him, and wearing a wedding band crafted from the nails of his cross. Under the protection of his grace, we are safe from whatever may threaten us, for nothing and no one can separate us from his love.

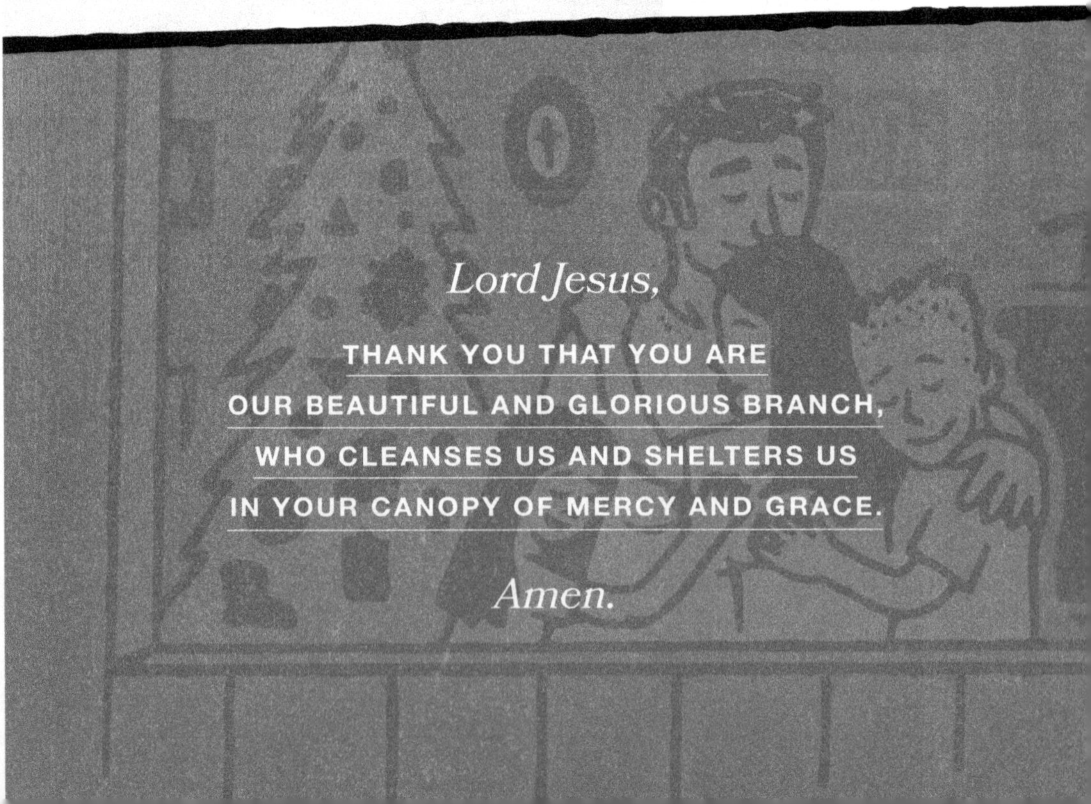

Lord Jesus,

THANK YOU THAT YOU ARE
OUR BEAUTIFUL AND GLORIOUS BRANCH,
WHO CLEANSES US AND SHELTERS US
IN YOUR CANOPY OF MERCY AND GRACE.

Amen.

Our Beloved God of Dread

ISAIAH 8:13-17

But the Lord of hosts, him you shall honor as holy. Let him be your fear, and let him be your dread. And he will become a sanctuary and a stone of offense and a rock of stumbling to both houses of Israel, a trap and a snare to the inhabitants of Jerusalem. And many shall stumble on it. They shall fall and be broken; they shall be snared and taken. Bind up the testimony; seal the teaching among my disciples. I will wait for the Lord, who is hiding his face from the house of Jacob, and I will hope in him.

We find these verses smackdab in the middle of Isaiah's prophecy of the destruction of the northern kingdom of Israel (and near destruction of Judah). The prophet's reminder to the people of Judah, to those who follow the Lord, is not to walk in the way of the Assyrians, nor fear what they fear (vv. 11-12). Instead,"Let [God] be your fear and let him be your dread," he says. This doesn't sound much like a comforting promise. "Our Beloved God of Dread" isn't something you'll see cross-stiched on a pillow or a Christmas tree ornament, nor is it likely to be the title of any Christmas carols sung this year.

But before we move past this admonition, let's first consider exactly what it means to fear and dread:

To fear God, is to honor him as holy (v. 13).
To fear God, is to know God as our Creator (Psalm 33).
To fear God, is to trust him above all else.

Isaiah says "Let him be your fear," meaning fear and dread in God alone, for he alone is powerful enough to not only conquer our enemies, but to save us from destruction. **He alone is a secure and safe dwelling place.** Trust in God, and you have no need to fear anything else.

As we plod through the Advent season, fearful of not meeting end-of-the-year quotas, of not getting the perfect Christmas gift for our kid in time, or perhaps even of the time we'll spend alone while it seems everyone else is off together celebrating, remember that it is Jesus Christ - the swaddled babe who comes to us in bursts of tears and need of milk - who is our fear. We fear him because he is God, and we are not. And he comes not just to live, but to die for you and for me so that the wrath of God is satisfied that we might be reconciled with the Almighty, brought back into the house of Jacob.

Without him, we will fall and be broken. We will stumble on our works as a means to righteousness (Rom. 9:31-33). But with him and in him, we have sanctuary.

Dear Jesus,

THANK YOU FOR BEING BOTH OUR FEAR AND OUR SANCTUARY SO THAT WE CAN TRUST YOUR WORK ON THE CROSS TO OVERCOME OUR SIN, DEATH AND THE DEVIL.

Amen.

Christmas Carols for Eternity

ISAIAH 12:1-6

You will say in that day: "I will give thanks to you, O Lord, for though you were angry with me, your anger turned away, that you might comfort me. "Behold, God is my salvation; I will trust, and will not be afraid; for the Lord God is my strength and my song, and he has become my salvation." With joy you will draw water from the wells of salvation. And you will say in that day: "Give thanks to the Lord, call upon his name, make known his deeds among the peoples, proclaim that his name is exalted. "Sing praises to the Lord, for he has done gloriously; let this be made known in all the earth. Shout, and sing for joy, O inhabitant of Zion, for great in your midst is the Holy One of Israel."

Advent and Christmas afford us the opportunity to sing some of the church's greatest hymns. These songs are a glimpse of that glorious chorus we'll join when Christ comes again. His first coming most certainly gave us reason to sing! For Jesus came in blessing to pay for our sins on the cross, shedding his blood to satisfy the wrath of God. He turned God's anger away from us by taking it upon himself, and in exchange, gave us the comfort of forgiveness and reconciliation with God (v. 1).

With God's anger gone, we have no reason to fear. Fear leads to silence. You try to hide from what frightens you, because you don't want to capture any attention. But there is nothing to fear from God on account of Jesus' incarnation and passion. The Lord God is now our song that we sing! (v. 2)

Imagine going Christmas caroling through your neighborhood. After you ring the doorbell of each home, the residents are delighted by your presence. In fact, they are prepared for you before you even arrive. They have cookies and cocoa waiting as they invite you to their home for holiday cheer.

God's love for our singing is like that. He hears our song and opens the doors with joy and delight, which only drives us to sing more from the joy in our hearts! Have you ever noticed how much we sing when we go to the Lord's Supper? There are songs before in preparation for the meal, songs sung during the reception, and songs as we conclude the service. Songs of faith, hope, and love. Songs of joy for the gifts of Christ's body and blood placed on our lips. Lips that take, eat, and cannot be stopped from singing! **God has welcomed you into his home with gifts to give! How can we keep from singing?**

That song of praise will know no end. When Christ comes again, we will join with all the resurrected saints and the armies of angels in our eternal home, singing praises to our Lord. "For he has done gloriously; let this be made known in all the earth!" (v. 5) Make it known in the earth indeed - perhaps you can even start in your neighborhood with Christmas caroling.

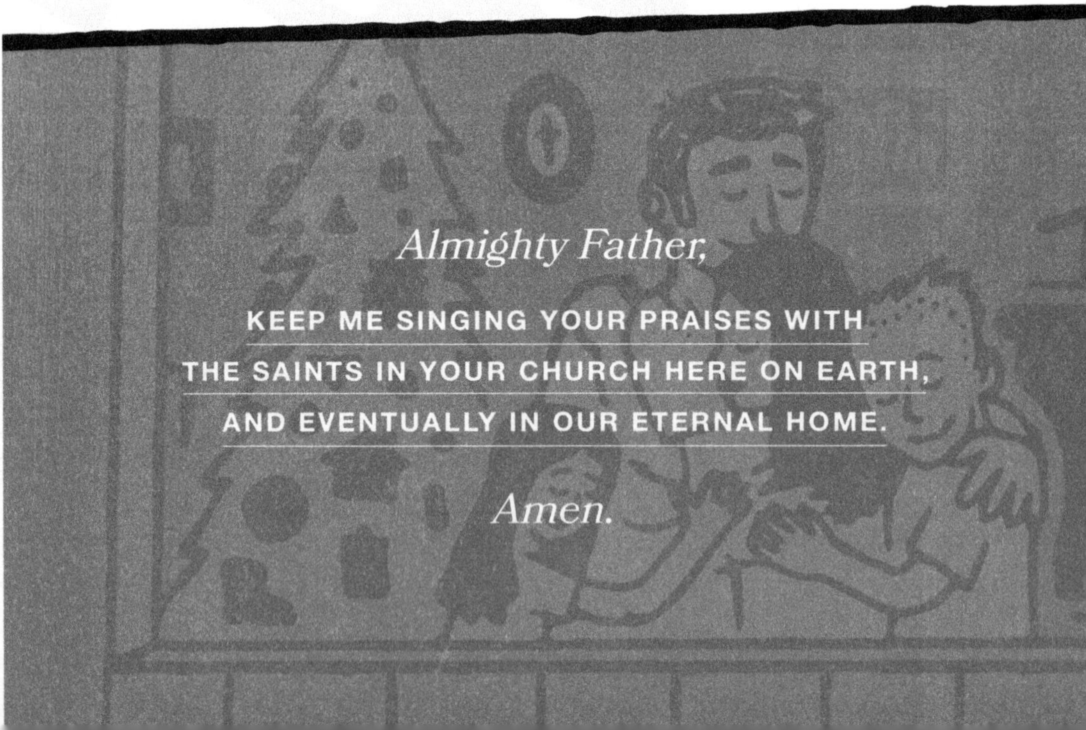

Almighty Father,

KEEP ME SINGING YOUR PRAISES WITH THE SAINTS IN YOUR CHURCH HERE ON EARTH, AND EVENTUALLY IN OUR ETERNAL HOME.

Amen.

The Thieving Party Host

ISAIAH 25:6-9

On this mountain the Lord of hosts will make for all peoples a feast of rich food, a feast of well-aged wine, of rich food full of marrow, of aged wine well refined. And he will swallow up on this mountain the covering that is cast over all peoples, the veil that is spread over all nations. He will swallow up death forever; and the Lord God will wipe away tears from all faces, and the reproach of his people he will take away from all the earth, for the Lord has spoken. It will be said on that day, "Behold, this is our God; we have waited for him, that he might save us. This is the Lord; we have waited for him; let us be glad and rejoice in his salvation."

Rich food and well-aged wine are wonderful things to receive from God. The heavenly feast on the mountain of the Lord, which God himself hosts, is certainly a promise worth clinging to. However, at this house party it's not just food and drink we receive. **Our God is a giver of endless gifts. He won't let us leave the party without bestowing on us the very best.** He has given us his own righteousness, adopted us as his children, and gifted us eternal life. But God is unlike any host we know. For before he gives, he takes like a thief who comes in the night (1 Thess. 5:2).

Why would the Scriptures describe Jesus as a thief? Isaiah 25 gives us the answer. It is because of everything he takes away. Jesus steals the death we have earned and swallows it up. Jesus wipes the tears from the faces of all who trust in him. Jesus takes away the reproach of brothers and sisters. He doesn't ask if you would like him to do these things, he just does them. Before Jesus gives, he takes. Before you are imputed with his righteousness, he is imputed with your sin.

Advent is about the arrival of the great stealer of all sin. In Christ, God has broken into our world and stolen everything that seeks to own and destroy us. Jesus is the long-awaited burglar of God, stealing all sin, shame, and death and bringing salvation to the world. Jesus is the holy party host who saves, but make no mistake, he is still a thief. He will not ask permission.

So this Advent, celebrate the arrival of this strange party host, who gives and takes away (Job 1:21). Let us rejoice and be glad that we are welcomed into this thief's home to receive his gifts.

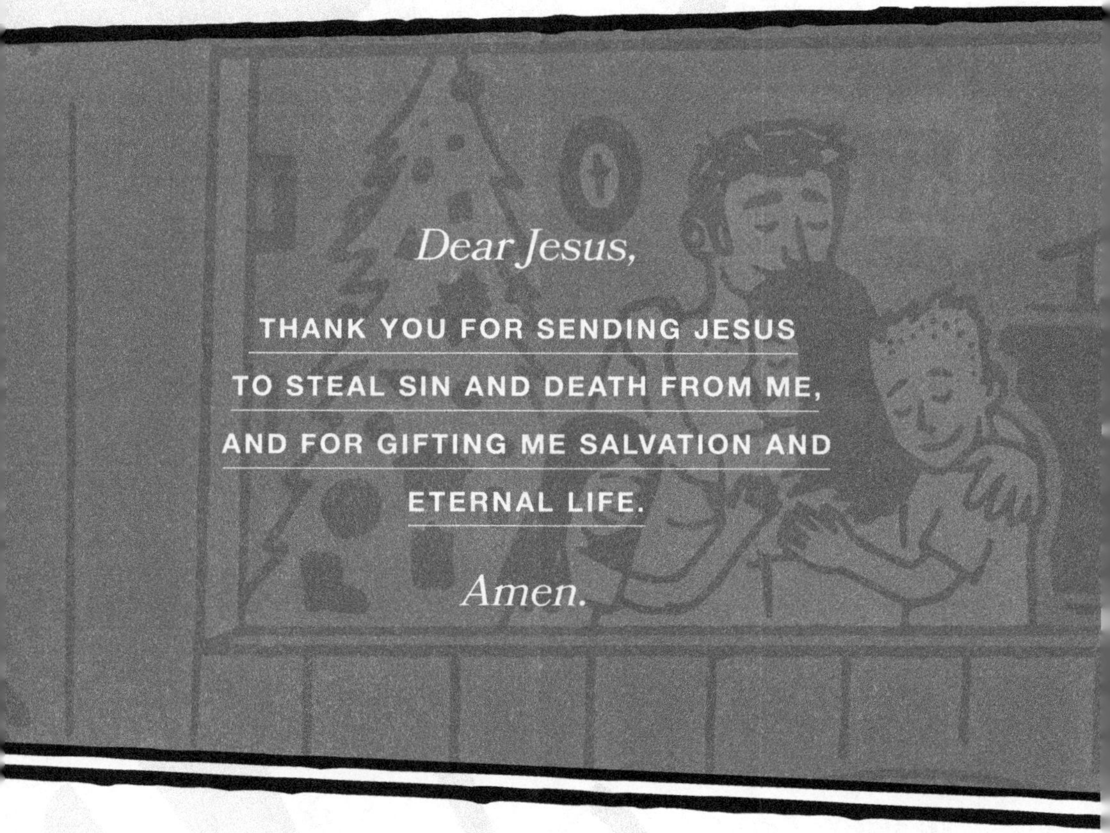

Dear Jesus,

THANK YOU FOR SENDING JESUS TO STEAL SIN AND DEATH FROM ME, AND FOR GIFTING ME SALVATION AND ETERNAL LIFE.

Amen.

The Word That Keeps Us in the Way

ISAIAH 30:19-21

For a people shall dwell in Zion, in Jerusalem; you shall weep no more. He will surely be gracious to you at the sound of your cry. As soon as he hears it, he answers you. And though the Lord give you the bread of adversity and the water of affliction, yet your Teacher will not hide himself anymore, but your eyes shall see your Teacher. And your ears shall hear a word behind you, saying, "This is the way, walk in it," when you turn to the right or when you turn to the left.

If you have children, you've undoubtedly found yourself at some point comforting a tearful toddler or a worked up preteen with some version of the phrase, "There is nothing to cry about." No doubt well-intentioned (and sometimes even effective), such words are not always as true as we would like them to be. Sometimes, it seems, there is actually *a lot* to cry about: pain, grief, sadness, and inexplicable suffering are a part of life no matter how young or old you are.

No one knows this better than our God, who, Isaiah tells us in chapter 30, not only hears our cries, but is gracious to answer them - even when we, through our rebellion and unbelief, are the very cause of them. And that's not all.

Not only does God answer our cries, he makes a promise that those who belong to him shall one day dwell in Zion - the heavenly city - where "you shall weep no more" (v. 9). **He is preparing a home for us where he doesn't simply comfort us in sadness, but the root cause of any and all tears ceases to exist.**

These are the words of promise the teacher, Isaiah, gives to the people of Judah as they face oppression from the Assyrians. But they are the words of promise for us as well, words which are sure because they have already been fulfilled through

Christ who came to not just comfort our affliction, but to end it once and for all. These words, spoken then by the prophet Isaiah and repeated now for us, surround us, whispering, "This is the way, walk in it." Christ came to be the way, gently ushering us forward with his promises until he comes again. His word reminds us that we are both in him while also daily walking ever closer to him. And very soon, we will dwell with him forever, where sin and tears are but a distant memory.

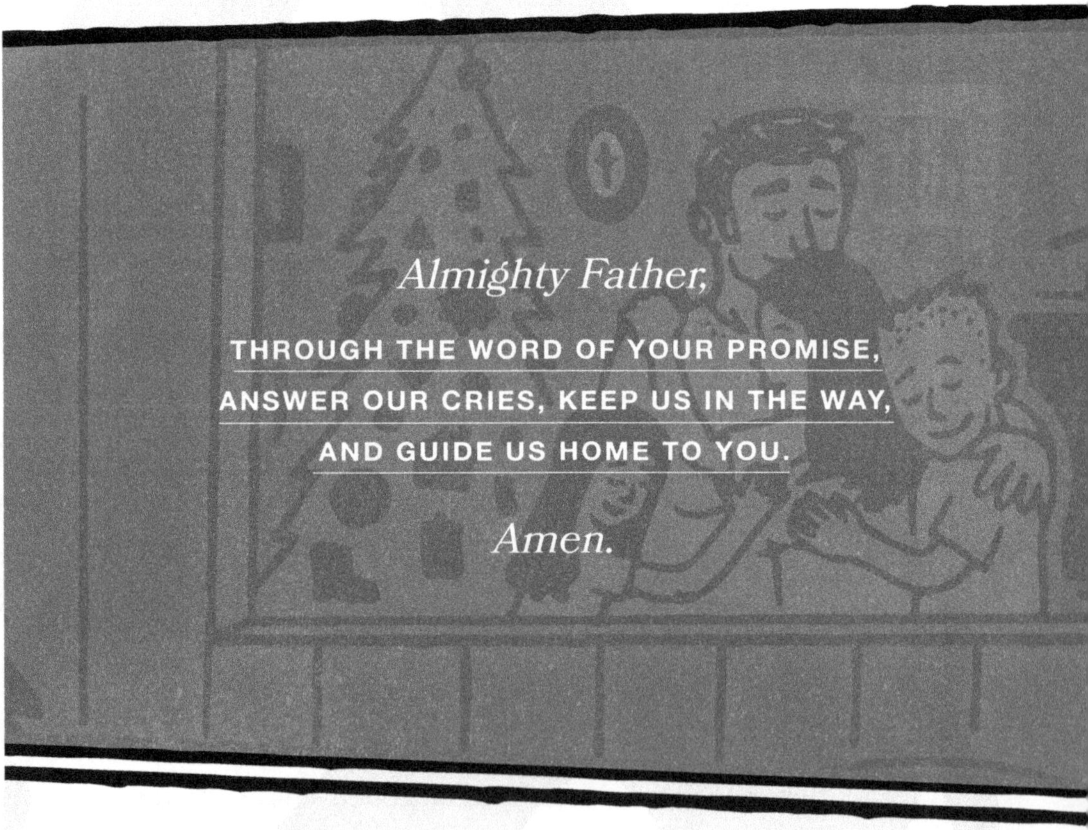

Almighty Father,

THROUGH THE WORD OF YOUR PROMISE,
ANSWER OUR CRIES, KEEP US IN THE WAY,
AND GUIDE US HOME TO YOU.

Amen.

Sing for Joy!

ISAIAH 49:8-13

Thus says the Lord: "In a time of favor I have answered you; in a day of salvation I have helped you; I will keep you and give you as a covenant to the people, to establish the land, to apportion the desolate heritages, saying to the prisoners, 'Come out,' to those who are in darkness, 'Appear.' They shall feed along the ways; on all bare heights shall be their pasture; they shall not hunger or thirst, neither scorching wind nor sun shall strike them, for he who has pity on them will lead them, and by springs of water will guide them. And I will make all my mountains a road, and my highways shall be raised up. Behold, these shall come from afar, and behold, these from the north and from the west, and these from the land of Syene." Sing for joy, O heavens, and exult, O earth; break forth, O mountains, into singing! For the Lord has comforted his people and will have compassion on his afflicted.

On the eve of our Lord's nativity celebration, as we anticipate gazing with wonder into that manger of mercy, what do we expect to see? A swaddled baby? Yes. The God who has become one of us? Yes.

We also see the embodiment of all our hope. "Thus says the Lord: 'In a time of favor I have answered you; in a day of salvation I have helped you; I will keep you and give you as a covenant to the people…" (v. 8). There in the manger is the new and better covenant—one with arms and legs, a heart and soul, body and blood.

This Son of Mary and Son of God says to those imprisoned in death, "Come out," and to those who are in darkness, "Appear and walk in the light." This Good Shepherd, who will feed us along the way. We shall neither hunger nor thirst, neither scorching wind nor sun shall strike us, for Jesus lovingly leads us by springs of living water. No lamb does he leave behind, for each of us is too precious for him to lose.

No matter how far we are from him, he is near to us, to bring us home to the Father. From blown-up lives and pits of despair, from all the dark and dismal dungeons of the soul where we think all hope is lost, **he is there to pick us up, throw us over his shoulder, and carry us back to where we belong.**

"So sing for joy, O heavens, and exult, O earth; break forth, O mountains, into singing! For the Lord Jesus has comforted us and will have compassion on his afflicted" (v. 13). He indeed is all our hope, all our confidence, all the promises of God come true.

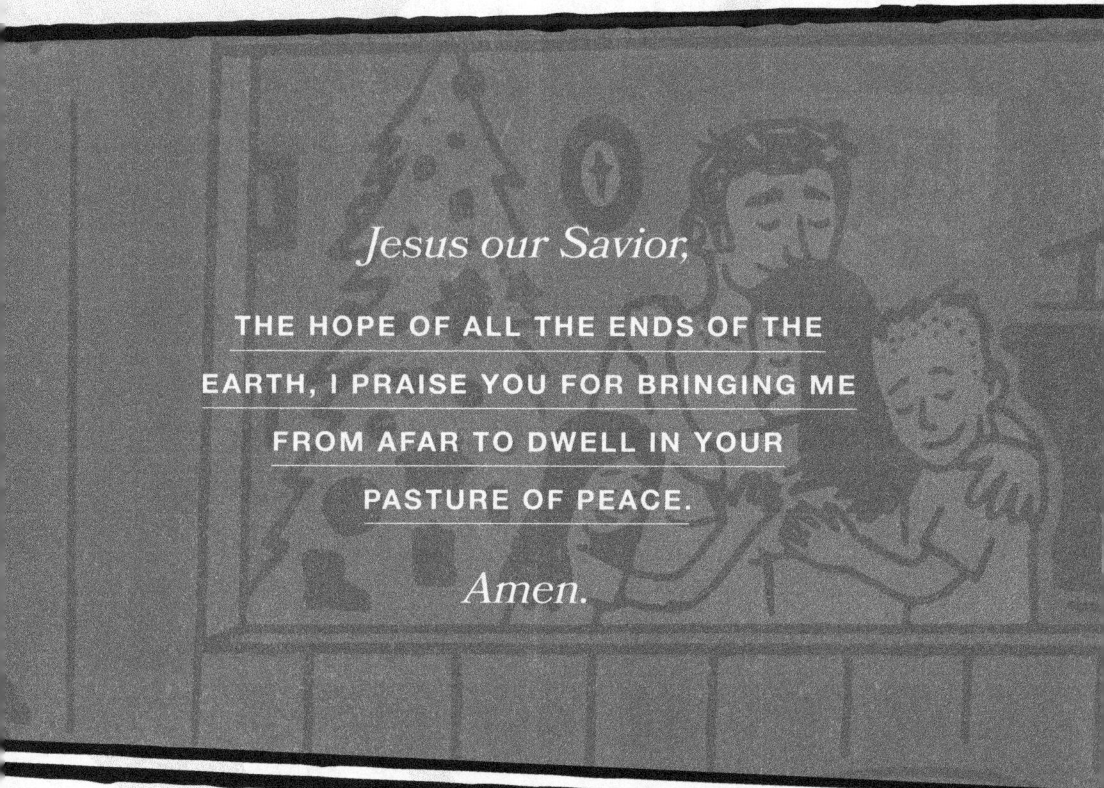

Jesus our Savior,

THE HOPE OF ALL THE ENDS OF THE EARTH, I PRAISE YOU FOR BRINGING ME FROM AFAR TO DWELL IN YOUR PASTURE OF PEACE.

Amen.

The Broad-Shouldered Baby

ISAIAH 9:6-7

For to us a child is born, to us a son is given; and the government shall be upon his shoulder, and his name shall be called Wonderful Counselor, Mighty God, Everlasting Father, Prince of Peace. Of the increase of his government and of peace there will be no end, on the throne of David and over his kingdom, to establish it and to uphold it with justice and with righteousness from this time forth and forevermore. The zeal of the Lord of hosts will do this.

If you were making plans to save the world and needed to pick a hero, you definitely wouldn't choose a baby. But God did.

The first five verses of this chapter of Isaiah function like an extended introduction to the Messiah, building the hype and ratcheting up expectations. It turns out that, for a baby, his resume is pretty impressive: He's going to reverse the fate of his people (v. 1), shine a light in the darkness (v. 2), raise the spirits of an exiled nation (v. 3), and overthrow the enemy (vv. 4-5). After such a vivid description, we might expect Hercules, Beowulf, or Superman to enter stage right. But as the curtain draws back, we are shocked to discover that God's Messiah is not wearing a cape, but diapers: "For to us a child is born, to us a son is given" (v. 6a).

To a world in bondage to sin, God sends a baby.

But this isn't any ordinary baby. Spiritually-speaking, this baby has shoulders broad enough to carry the White House, the Kremlin, and Buckingham Palace combined without breaking a sweat (v. 6b). This baby knows just what to do in every situation ("Wonderful Counselor"), possesses burly biceps ("Mighty God"), is without beginning or end ("Everlasting Father"), and brings rest to the weary by establishing his kingdom and ruling with justice ("Prince of Peace"). All this because the shoulders of the baby-king are broad enough to carry you–even in your weakness: "My grace is sufficient for you, for my power is made perfect in weakness" (2 Cor. 12:9).

The kingdom of God comes swaddled in weakness rather than strength. It is not of this world. It is a place where peace rather than anxiety gets the final word, and where all things are as they should be. **Through faith, Christians become card-carrying members of the kingdom of God.** We are, spiritually-speaking, adopted and re-homed into our Heavenly Father's household. Our gracious Father gives us a new status and a new relationship: We are now his beloved sons and daughters, children of a mercifully zealous (v. 7) Father who always sets an extra spot at the table for his children and always keeps the light on.

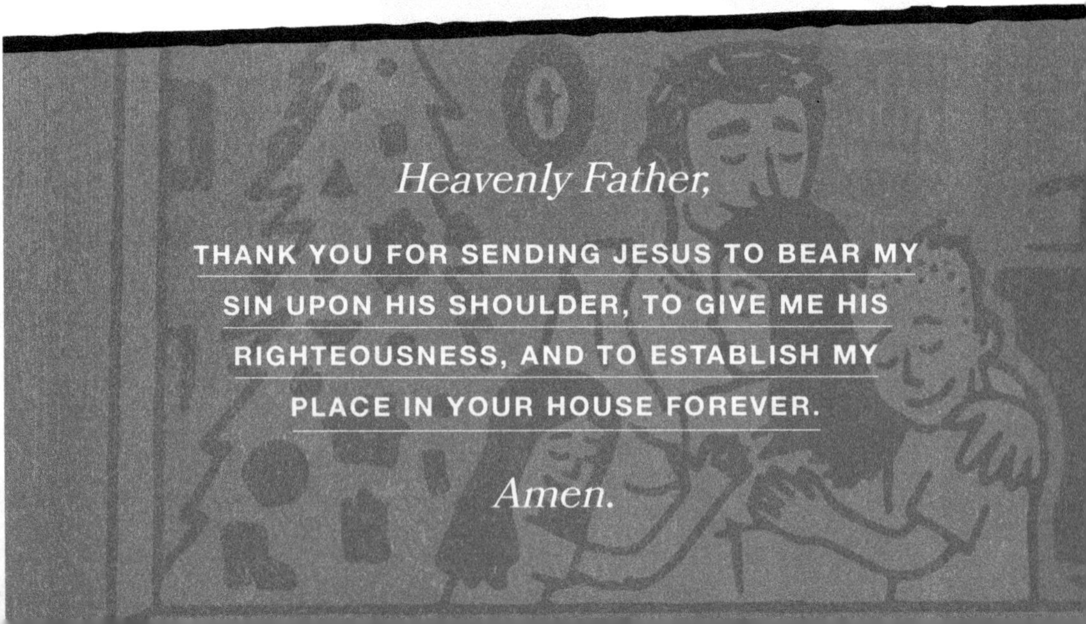

Heavenly Father,

THANK YOU FOR SENDING JESUS TO BEAR MY SIN UPON HIS SHOULDER, TO GIVE ME HIS RIGHTEOUSNESS, AND TO ESTABLISH MY PLACE IN YOUR HOUSE FOREVER.

Amen.

www.ingramcontent.com/pod-product-compliance
Lightning Source LLC
LaVergne TN
LVHW041158071125
825119LV00005B/9